O is for Orkney

by Britt Harcus

O is for Orkney

Published by Britt Harcus
First Edition
ISBN - 9780995474833

www.brittharcus.com

This book is dedicated to Robbie and Erlend x

A is for

AuK

Little Auk

B is for BULL

is for **Cow**

D is for DRY STONE DYKE

F is for

FROG

G is for GOOSE

H is for HARE

I is for

ISLANDS

J

is for

JELLYFISH

K is for KIRKWALL

is for

M is for

MOUSE

is for

N

NORTH
RONALDSAY
SHEEP

OYSTERCATCHER
is for

P

is for

PuFFIN

is for

Quail

is for

RAVEN

is for SEAL

T

is for

TRACTOR

U is for

UMBRELLA

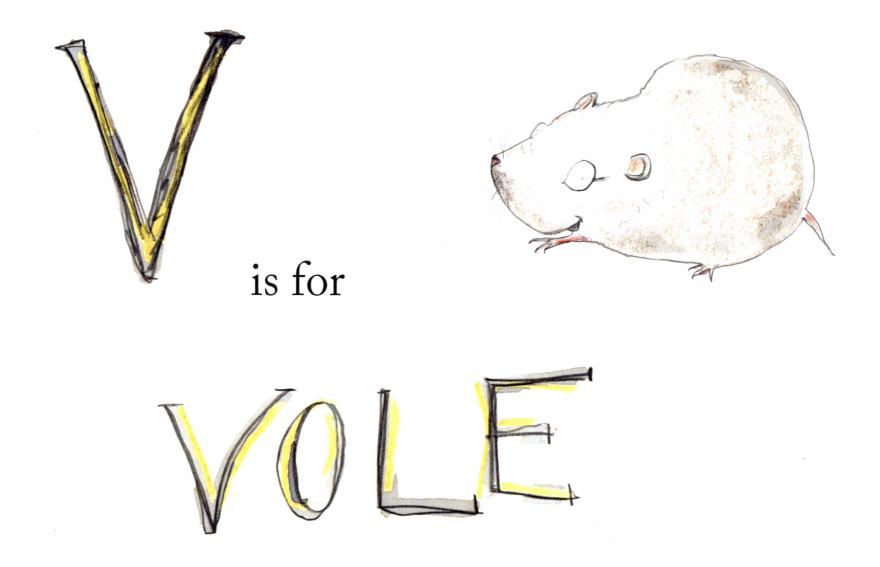

V is for

VOLE

W is for

WHALE

X is for EXTRA LAYERS

Y is for YESNABY

Z is for

Some further Orcadian words and their meanings...

Aye aye - Hello
Groatie buckie - Tiny shell
Neep - Turnip
Peedie - Small
Tatties - Potatoes

Maybe you can think of some more
or create your own A-Z for where you live.
I would love to see your artwork.
Thank you,

Britt x

Other Britt books...
'Janice and the Special Breakfast' &
'Made Up Muck?'
Visit www.brittharcus.com
Follow Britt Harcus on Instagram, Facebook & Twitter
Thank you

ORKNEY, SCOTLAND, UK

Britt Harcus is a popular and talented Scottish illustrator, writer and storyteller. Britt studied at NCAD, Dublin and Lahti Polytechnic, Finland before returning back home to the beautiful Orkney Islands. Her first publication was 'Made Up Muck?' back in 2005. Since then Britt has gathered an impressive portfolio of clients in the private and commercial sector. When she is not illustrating books, Britt loves spending time with her family and horses.

Lightning Source UK Ltd.
Milton Keynes UK
UKRC031006290622
405125UK00001B/5